CW01163434

Original title:
A New Chapter

Copyright © 2024 Swan Charm
All rights reserved.

Author: Olivia Oja
ISBN HARDBACK: 978-9916-89-976-2
ISBN PAPERBACK: 978-9916-89-977-9
ISBN EBOOK: 978-9916-89-978-6

A Tapestry of Grace and Renewal

In the silence of dawn we lift our eyes,
Blessings fall softly like whispers in skies.
Threads of hope woven, each prayer a strand,
In the fabric of life, we find His hand.

Grace awakened in hearts that once strayed,
In the warmth of His love, all darkness betrayed.
Renewed in His light, we rise from the dust,
Faith unbroken, in Him we trust.

Guardians of Tomorrow's Dreams

With eyes full of wonder, we gaze at the stars,
In the night's gentle hush, we surrender our scars.
Dreams are the seedlings, planted by grace,
Guardians of light, we strive to embrace.

The paths that we wander, with courage we tread,
Nurtured by faith, our spirits are fed.
Each step a commitment, a choice made anew,
Together in purpose, in love we pursue.

The Meeting of Paths and Faith

Two roads converging in the light of day,
In the heart of the traveler, choices lay.
Faith is the compass, guiding us near,
At the crossroads of life, His voice we hear.

With every decision, our hopes intertwine,
In the tapestry woven, our destinies shine.
We walk hand in hand, no fear in our hearts,
In the meeting of paths, true love imparts.

The Spirit's Trail of Discovery

In the wilderness vast, where shadows may creep,
The Spirit calls softly, promises keep.
Each step a revelation, a glimpse of His grace,
In the depths of our journey, we find our place.

Through valleys of doubt, in storms we press on,
The light of His presence dispels the dark dawn.
Every whisper, a treasure, each moment a gift,
In the trail of discovery, our spirits uplift.

Signs of the Divine Tapestry

In the morning light, the whispers start,
Threads of grace weave through the heart.
Nature's song, a sacred hymn,
In every shadow, the lights grow dim.

Mountains rise, hands to the sky,
Every peak, a place to fly.
Rivers flow with wisdom's reach,
In silence, the spirit can teach.

Stars above in the velvet night,
Each a beacon, a guiding light.
Moments shared beneath the moon,
Divine presence, a soft tune.

In kindness shown, the truth revealed,
Through loving acts, the heart is healed.
Every gaze, a chance to see,
Signs of love in you and me.

We gather close, the circle formed,
United in love, our spirits warmed.
In deep prayer, we find our way,
Tapestry unfolds, come what may.

Blessings of the Unwritten

In the stillness, stories flow,
Pages blank with hopes to grow.
Whispers of fate, softly caress,
In every moment, a deep blessedness.

The dawn breaks, a canvas bright,
With strokes of faith, we paint the light.
Unseen blessings, we embrace,
In every smile, the world's grace.

Journeying through the paths unknown,
Each step taken, we are not alone.
From trials faced, the spirit soars,
Through pain and joy, our heart explores.

Life unfolds like petals new,
Unwritten words, a sacred view.
In every tear, a joyful sign,
Blessings waiting, yours and mine.

Together we stand, hand in hand,
In unity, we understand.
The unwritten blessings, pure and free,
Guide our hearts to eternity.

Chronicles of the Spirit's Ascent

From deep within, the journey starts,
The spirit rises, igniting hearts.
Each moment lived, a step we'll take,
In love's embrace, we gently wake.

In quietude, the truths arise,
Veils lifted, revealing skies.
Mountains climbed, yet valleys near,
In every breath, the essence clear.

Time flows like rivers in the night,
Leaving traces of sacred light.
Chronicles echo, stories fair,
Guiding souls to the purest air.

Through shadows cast, our faith is strong,
With each challenge, we belong.
Ascent unfolds on this divine ride,
In oneness, we walk side by side.

The spirit's call, a timeless gift,
In love's embrace, our spirits lift.
Across the skies, our voices sing,
Chronicles of what hope can bring.

The Holy Pathway Emerges

In shadows cast by doubt and fear,
The holy pathway starts to clear.
Every step, a purpose known,
In the silence, our truth is sown.

Through trials faced, the heart is tried,
In moments still, we abide.
With faith as our guiding star,
The pathway shines, no matter how far.

The call of love, it echoes wide,
In every soul, the light resides.
Hand in hand, we walk this road,
Together lifting each heavy load.

The sacred journey, a winding mile,
With every hardship, let's find our smile.
Hope unfolds as the dawn breaks free,
The holy pathway leads to thee.

Together we rise, hearts intertwined,
In every challenge, strength we find.
The journey sings, and our spirits soar,
On the holy pathway, forevermore.

Ashes to Radiance

From ashes we rise, with spirits renewed,
In shadows of sorrow, His light we pursue.
He lifts us from darkness, with grace from above,
Transforming our trials to blessings of love.

In faith we find hope, as we walk on this way,
Each step a reminder of His guiding sway.
With hearts ever open, we seek His embrace,
From dust unto glory, we find our place.

The Seraphim's New Song

The seraphim sing with voices so warm,
Their wings like a breeze, a holy swarm.
In praise of the Father, they chant day and night,
A melody woven in divine light.

Their notes swirl around us, lifting our souls,
Through trials and triumphs, His power consoles.
In harmony's dance, we join their sweet prayer,
United in worship, our burdens laid bare.

Radiant Horizons Await

O'er radiant horizons, our hearts set ablaze,
With visions of glory, we walk in His ways.
Through valleys of struggle, His promise shines bright,
Guiding our footsteps, with love as our light.

Each moment a gift, from heaven above,
In peace we will dwell, in His infinite love.
As dawn breaks the darkness, our spirits take flight,
For with Him beside us, all wrongs turn to right.

Stars in the Heavens Reflected

The stars in the heavens, a celestial choir,
Each twinkle a whisper of His world's desire.
Reflected in us, His image divine,
We dance in the darkness, our hearts ever shine.

In starlight we gather, with spirits entwined,
To seek out the truth, with our eyes truly blind.
In night’s gentle warmth, we find our way home,
As sparks of His love through the cosmos we roam.

The Sacred Bond of Resilience

In trials deep and shadows cast,
We rise anew from pain amassed.
With faith as strong, we find our way,
A sacred bond, come what may.

In every tear, a lesson learned,
Through every storm, our spirits burned.
United hearts in strength abide,
Together we will turn the tide.

When the night is dark and long,
We sing of hope, a steadfast song.
With hands held high, we face the dawn,
In sacred trust, we carry on.

Through valleys low and mountains high,
We lift our voices to the sky.
In the embrace of love we grow,
Resilience blooms, our hearts aglow.

So let us walk this path of grace,
In every challenge, find our place.
For in the trials we endure,
The sacred bond will keep us pure.

Charting a Celestial Course

Beneath the stars, our spirits soar,
With every dream, we seek for more.
A compass set to guide the way,
In cosmic dance, we find our sway.

The heavens speak in whispers soft,
In sacred paths, our souls lift off.
To chart the course through light and shade,
Together, in love, we will invade.

Through galaxies, our spirits glide,
In unity, we will abide.
With faith as our celestial guide,
We navigate the vast, wide tide.

In every heartbeat, starlight glows,
The essence of what faith bestows.
With open hearts, we journey far,
Embracing dreams, our guiding star.

So let us sail on winds of grace,
Through tempests fierce, we'll find our place.
In every challenge, we'll explore,
Charting a course forevermore.

In the Stillness of New Horizons

In quiet dawn, the world awakes,
A canvas fresh, the heart forsakes.
With every breath, new visions rise,
In stillness found beneath the skies.

The sun ascends, a golden hue,
In tranquil moments, whispers true.
With open hearts, we greet the day,
As new horizons pave the way.

Embrace the calm that fills the air,
In every pause, a sacred prayer.
From silence blooms, the spirit's song,
In stillness, we find where we belong.

With every step towards the light,
We cast aside our fears of night.
In unity, we take our stand,
In new horizons, hand in hand.

So let us walk with faith anew,
In sacred trust, our spirits grew.
For in stillness, every soul ignites,
New horizons, shining bright.

The Whisper of Hope's Unfolding

In shadows cast, a soft voice calls,
Through darkest nights, a light enthralls.
With every whisper, hope reclaims,
A gentle spark that fans the flames.

In trials faced, we find the grace,
A tender touch, a warm embrace.
With hearts open, we seek to find,
The endless love that binds all kind.

In quiet moments, faith takes flight,
Illuminating paths so bright.
With every breath, we rise and sing,
The melody that hope will bring.

As petals bloom in springtime's glow,
Our spirits dance, we learn to grow.
In every heartbeat, visions clear,
The whisper speaks, our purpose near.

So let us listen to the sound,
Of hope's unfolding all around.
For in each moment, love will guide,
Through every storm, we shall abide.

The Embrace of Every Breath

In the stillness of the dawn, we rise,
Each breath a gift from the skies.
With whispers of hope, our hearts align,
In gratitude's glow, our souls entwine.

In every exhale, a prayer is sent,
A sacred moment, divinely meant.
The essence of life, in harmony flows,
A dance of existence, where true love grows.

With every heartbeat, the spirit sings,
Awakening joy in the simplest things.
The universe breathes, a rhythm profound,
In the embrace of each breath, we are found.

Wings of the Spirit Taking Flight

Awake, arise, let your spirit soar,
On the wings of faith, we search for more.
Through trials and storms, our spirits ascend,
In the light of belief, our hearts mend.

With courage like fire, we rise above,
Embracing the power, the gift of love.
In the tapestry woven by heavenly thread,
We find our purpose, where angels tread.

As we glide through the skies, pure and bright,
The wings of the spirit embrace the light.
In unity's fold, our dreams take flight,
Together we journey, hearts burning bright.

From Shadows to the Sacred Light

Beneath the shadows, the spirit weeps,
Yet in the darkness, a promise keeps.
With each tear shed, a memory glows,
The path to the sacred, through struggle grows.

Emerging from fears, we seek the dawn,
A dance of redemption, where hope is born.
In the embrace of light, we shed our chains,
A symphony rises from heart's refrains.

With open arms, the universe calls,
From shadows to light, love never stalls.
In the journey of souls, we find our way,
Towards the sacred, where we long to stay.

Treading the Path of Grace

Step by step, on this sacred road,
With faith as our compass, we lighten the load.
In the depths of grace, we find our song,
A melody sweet, where we all belong.

Through valleys and peaks, in the dance of time,
We walk in harmony, our spirits climb.
With kindness as armor, we gather the brave,
Together we flourish, the lost we save.

As rivers of love, our pathway unfolds,
In the warmth of compassion, our journey molds.
Treading the path, in unity's grace,
We walk hand in hand, in this holy space.

A Pilgrimage of Hope

In the shadows, faith takes flight,
With each step, a guiding light.
Winds of grace, whispering near,
Carrying hearts through doubt and fear.

Paths may twist, and stones may rise,
Yet, through trials, we seek the skies.
Hands united, souls ablaze,
We walk this journey, sing His praise.

The mountain high, the valley low,
In every heartbeat, love will grow.
Strength in numbers, together we tread,
Finding solace where angels led.

Light the way, oh Holy guide,
With every moment, here abide.
In unity we rise and strive,
In the pilgrimage, we come alive.

Hope will echo through the night,
Shining brighter, the truth in sight.
Heaven's promise, sweet and clear,
We'll reach the dawn, forever near.

The Song of the Heart’s Ascent

Lifted spirits, voices soar,
In sacred hymns, we seek for more.
Every note a prayer released,
In the stillness, joy increased.

Mountains echo, valleys respond,
In this journey, we grow fond.
With each lyric, souls align,
In harmony, Your love does shine.

Strains of mercy, chords of grace,
In this refuge, we find our place.
Yearning hearts, together we sing,
In the ascent, new life will spring.

Through trials and triumphs, we hear,
The melody that draws us near.
In the rhythm of faith, we trust,
As our spirits rise, we must.

Oh, sweet song, forever flow,
In the heart's ascent, love will grow.
With every breath, we lift our praise,
In the song of life, we find our ways.

Navigating the Waters of Faith

Gentle tides, a guiding star,
In the waters, we journey far.
With faith as our steadfast sail,
Through stormy seas, we shall not fail.

Waves may crash, and winds may roar,
Yet, we trust the Lord's safe shore.
Hearts anchored deep, no fear shall bind,
In the ocean vast, His love we find.

Oceans call with whispers sweet,
In every ebb, a chance to meet.
Streams of mercy, flowing free,
Guiding all, eternally.

Rowing forth, hand in hand,
In this voyage, we understand.
Navigating with hearts ablaze,
In His presence, we find our ways.

For every trial, a lesson learned,
In the waters, His flame burns.
Faith will carry us through the night,
To shores of hope, into the light.

In the Garden of New Dawn

In the garden, blossoms bright,
Morning dew, pure and light.
Each petal tells a tale of grace,
Under Heaven's kind embrace.

Seeds of change, in soil they rest,\nWith whispered prayers, we are blessed.
Sunrise break, a brand new start,
In the stillness, joy takes part.

Beneath the branches, shadows fall,
In serenity, we heed the call.
Nature's choir, a sacred tune,
Awakens hearts, beneath the moon.

With gentle hands, we tend and sow,
In this garden, love will grow.
Through trials faced, and joys embraced,
In His presence, we are graced.

In the garden, hope remains,
Through every loss, and all the gains.
As dawn unfolds, our spirits soar,
In the garden, forevermore.

Echoes of the Risen Path

In shadows deep, the whispers call,
A guiding hand through trials small.
Faith leads us on, a steady line,
With every step, the light will shine.

Through valleys low, and mountains high,
The heart's true song will never die.
Hope's gentle voice, in stormy nights,
Reminds the soul of heavenly sights.

Embrace the grace, let burdens cease,
In humble prayer, we find our peace.
With open hearts, we seek to grow,
In love's embrace, our spirits flow.

Eternal truth, a sacred gift,
In every soul, the spirits lift.
United we stand, in faith we trust,
In echoes loud, our hearts combust.

To paths unknown, we bravely tread,
Each step a prayer, with love we're fed.
A journey blessed, divine and bright,
Together we walk, in holy light.

Sanctuary of the Spirit's Light

In quiet spaces, whispers dwell,
A sanctuary, where spirits swell.
Beneath the stars, in velvet night,
The soul ignites with heavenly light.

With every breath, a prayer we make,
In love's sweet bond, the dawn will break.
Hearts intertwined, in sacred trust,
In kindness shared, our spirits rust.

Through trials faced, in darkness found,
The spirit's voice, our hearts surround.
In gentle grace, we rise anew,
Awakening spirit, pure and true.

Each tear released, a sacred flow,
The rivers of faith begin to grow.
With open arms, we share the light,
In this sanctuary, hearts take flight.

Together we stand, in joy and pain,
In unity bound, we break the chain.
A promise kept, through endless years,
In this hallowed space, we cast our fears.

Awakening the Divine Light

In dawn's embrace, we rise and sing,
With every breath, the spirit's wing.
Awakening souls, in love's delight,
The heart ignites, a sacred light.

From ashes deep, new life will bloom,
In shadows cast, dispel the gloom.
Every moment, a gift divine,
In gratitude, our hearts entwine.

The call of truth, a gentle sound,
In silence found, our hopes abound.
With faith as guide, we venture forth,
To share the light, a blessed worth.

In every trial, our strength refined,
In unity, our spirits bind.
A tapestry of grace we weave,
In love's embrace, we learn, believe.

Together we rise, hands clasped in prayer,
The light within, a flame we share.
With every heartbeat, a promise made,
In awakening's rise, no fear will fade.

The Sacred Turning of Pages

In sacred books, the wisdom glows,
Each page a story, the spirit knows.
With ink of faith, and love's embrace,
We turn the pages, find our place.

Through ancient words, the truth revealed,
In sacred texts, our wounds are healed.
The journey written, in light and shade,
In every chapter, hope is laid.

From Genesis bright, to Revelations wide,
The path of grace, in love we bide.
In prayerful hearts, we seek to learn,
With every turn, our spirits yearn.

With eyes of faith, we read the lines,
In every lesson, the spirit shines.
Together we gather, the stories told,
In sacred turning, we become bold.

In every heartbeat, the echo stays,
In this grand tale, we walk our ways.
With every page, a new dawn breaks,
In sacred turning, the light awakes.

From Tribulation to Triumph

In shadows deep, we seek the light,
Through trials faced, our spirits fight.
Each tear we shed, a seed will grow,
From aching hearts, new strength will flow.

In anguish met with faith's embrace,
We rise again, our fears erase.
With every step, our burdens lift,
In grace we find our souls' true gift.

The dawn breaks forth, our eyes anew,
With courage gained, we dare pursue.
From pain to peace, our journey shifts,
In life's embrace, the spirit lifts.

Through storms we weep, yet hope remains,
In every heart, love's truth sustains.
The path may twist, the night may fall,
Yet through it all, we heed love's call.

From tribulation to triumph bright,
Our hearts aflame, our visions white.
In unity, we walk as one,
Through darkest nights, we find the sun.

Serene Passages of the Soul

In stillness found, a whisper calls,
The sacred breath, where quiet falls.
With every pulse, a moment flows,
In harmony, the spirit knows.

Through valleys deep, and mountains high,
In peace we dwell, beneath the sky.
Each heartbeat sings a soft refrain,
In timeless grace, we learn the gain.

As rivers run, so do we seek,
The gentle touch, the love we speak.
With open hearts, in silence stood,
In tranquil shores, we find the good.

The moonlit path, a guiding light,
In shadows cast, we rise from night.
As stars align, the soul takes flight,
In sacred bonds, we reunite.

In serene passages, we roam,
For every heart shall find its home.
In unity, we are made whole,
A journey blessed, the sacred soul.

The Unveiling of the Heart’s Canvas

With gentle strokes, our spirits blend,
In colors bright, the heart transcends.
Each brush of fate paints love anew,
The canvas speaks, with every hue.

In shadows cast, we find the light,
Within the deep, we seek what's right.
The heart's true art lies bare and bold,
In every tale, a grace retold.

With open arms, we greet the view,
As vibrant dreams begin to brew.
Through trials faced, the beauty shines,
In every line, the soul defines.

The masterpiece unfolds with time,
A sacred dance, an endless rhyme.
In strokes of faith, we rise and fall,
The heart’s own song will lead us all.

In unveiling love, we find our place,
In every shade, divine embrace.
Through passion’s fire, our spirits race,
On this canvas, we seek His grace.

Journeying Through Sacred Time

In sacred moments, we intertwine,
Through winding paths, our hearts align.
With every breath, a prayer we weave,
In whispers soft, our souls believe.

Each passing hour, a gift bestowed,
In every step, we walk the road.
Through joy and pain, in love we trust,
In sacred time, our spirits must.

The clock may tick, yet we remain,
In timeless grace, we break the chain.
With faith we rise, our burdens cease,
In every trial, we find our peace.

As seasons change, our hearts will grow,
In every twist, new seeds we sow.
With open eyes, we see the signs,
In sacred time, our life assigns.

Journeying forth, to realms unseen,
In every moment, love's path is keen.
Through sacred time, our spirits soar,
In divine rhythm, forevermore.

The Sacred Rhythm of Turning Pages

In silence, the pages turn,
A whisper of the divine spark,
Each word, a prayer, a yearn,
Guiding souls through the dark.

The stories of old unfold,
In sacred light, they shine bright,
With wisdom, their truths are told,
A harmony born of the night.

Each chapter, a journey anew,
From struggle to grace we flow,
Embracing the love that is true,
In the heart, the sacred glow.

With every line, souls entwine,
In holy verse, they find peace,
United in the grand design,
A timeless gift that won't cease.

The rhythm of life, a sweet song,
Each turn a chance to embrace,
In the pages, we all belong,
Finding purpose in the grace.

The Beauty of Tomorrow's Gifts

In the dawn, the promise lies,
A canvas of hope, pure and bright,
With each sunrise, new dreams arise,
Guided by divine light.

Nature sings in vibrant tone,
With colors that dance and play,
Reminding us we're not alone,
As we cherish each day.

The wind carries whispers fair,
Of blessings that come our way,
Instilling a spirit rare,
In the heart's gentle sway.

With gratitude, let us create,
A tomorrow filled with grace,
Embracing love, never hate,
In every heart, a sacred place.

Together we weave our fate,
In harmony, we will rise,
Finding joy in what we cultivate,
Living under sacred skies.

Rewriting Destiny with Grace

In the stillness, change begins,
With each thought, we forge our path,
Transforming battles into wins,
Guided by love, not wrath.

The ink of faith flows strong,
On the parchment of the heart,
With every chord, a fervent song,
Creating a brand new start.

A tapestry of dreams we weave,
With threads of hope and light,
In unity, we dare believe,
Our future shining bright.

With gentle hands, let us mold,
The stories yet to be told,
Through love, our destinies unfold,
As the universe takes hold.

In the echoes of our choice,
Divine whispers remain true,
With every step, we hear the voice,
Of the sacred guiding you.

The Dawn of Spiritual Reckoning

Awake, O soul, and rise anew,
As the dawn breaks with soft light,
The truths of ages calling you,
To embrace your inner sight.

In the stillness, spirits stir,
With wisdom harsh yet kind,
A journey deep where hearts confer,
In the silence, love we find.

The veil of doubt begins to fade,
As clarity shines through,
In reverence, let us not evade,
The calling that is due.

Each moment, a chance to grow,
In the dance of the divine,
Through trials faced, we learn to flow,
In unity, hearts align.

As dawn ascends, so shall we,
Transcending pain and fear,
In this reckoning, we'll see,
Beyond the veil, the clear.

The Call of Sacred Wanderlust

In quiet dawn, a whispering light,
Calls the soul to seek and flight.
Footsteps trace on sacred ground,
In every heart, the truth is found.

Mountains high, and rivers wide,
Nature beckons, be our guide.
With open arms, we roam afar,
To touch the edge of every star.

Voices echo in the breeze,
A sacred song that never flees.
In every path, a lesson shines,
The wanderer's heart, forever pines.

Mysteries in shadows dwell,
Within each tale, a truth to tell.
Through valleys deep, our spirits soar,
We are the seekers, evermore.

Find the light in every tear,
With every step, we conquer fear.
The call of wanderlust is clear,
In sacred journeys, we draw near.

In the Arms of Infinite Possibility

In the stillness, dreams arise,
In quiet hearts, the visions lie.
Every thought a seed we plant,
In Divine soil, where hopes enchant.

A universe of open doors,
Limitless paths on endless shores.
In the pulse of cosmic grace,
We find a home in boundless space.

Time unfolds, a tender arc,
In every spark, the holy mark.
With every breath, a chance to rise,
To paint our lives in sacred skies.

In the whispers of the night,
The stars conspire, oh, such light!
Embrace the force of all that's true,
Infinite paths await for you.

Let courage be your guiding hand,
With faith, we journey toward the grand.
The universe, our faithful friend,
In every moment, love transcends.

The Holy Embrace of Change

In the shifting tides of time,
We find the rhythm, the sacred rhyme.
Every season, a sacred flow,
In changing winds, our spirits grow.

Leaves may fall, yet roots run deep,
In change, the promises we keep.
Through trials faced, and lessons learned,
In holy fires, our hearts are burned.

With each dawn, new colors wake,
In the hands of fate, we partake.
Transformation, a dance divine,
In every heartbeat, love will shine.

Let go of fears that clutch so tight,
In every ending, find the light.
The sacred ebb, the flow of grace,
In every turn, we find our place.

Embrace the waves, the sweet unknown,
In each step, let courage be sown.
A holy journey, we must share,
In change, we find our purpose there.

Shifting Sands of the Spirit

On shifting sands, our spirits tread,
In every grain, the truth is spread.
The desert winds, they whisper low,
Of ancient paths and wisdom's flow.

Through trials faced on barren land,
We understand, we take a stand.
With open hearts, we seek to know,
The sacred seeds that life will sow.

Mountains rise, and rivers bend,
In nature's dance, we start to mend.
Each challenge met, a step in grace,
In shifting sands, we find our place.

Feel the pulse of earth's embrace,
In every step, a holy trace.
The spirit whispers, loud and clear,
In life's great journey, we persevere.

When shadows fall, and doubts arrive,
Let faith ignite, and love revive.
With every dawn, our spirits sing,
In shifting sands, we take to wing.

The Journey of Becoming Whole

In shadows cast by doubt and fear,
We seek the light, our path made clear.
With every step, a lesson learned,
In hearts aflame, our spirits turned.

Through valleys deep and mountains high,
We lift our gaze, we learn to fly.
The whispers of the soul will guide,
In faith, in love, we must abide.

The journey writes our history,
In sacred scrolls, the mystery.
With open hearts, we dare to grow,
As we embrace the ebb and flow.

Each prayer, a breath, each breath, a song,
In sacred harmony, where we belong.
With every trial, our spirits soar,
Becoming whole, forevermore.

Together, hand in hand, we strive,
In love's embrace, we come alive.
The journey leads us ever near,
To sacred space, where hearts appear.

Walking on Holy Ground

With every step, the earth does sing,
A hymn of hope, a blossoming.
In silence deep, we hear the call,
As sacred light begins to fall.

The grasses sway, the branches bend,
In nature's arms, we find our friend.
With humbled hearts, we tread the trail,
On holy ground, we shall not fail.

Each moment holds a sacred boon,
The sun, the stars, the silver moon.
With open eyes, we see the grace,
Of life unfolding, a warm embrace.

As footsteps merge with ancient ways,
We find our truth in gentle rays.
With reverence, our spirits rise,
In unity beneath the skies.

Together on this sacred shore,
We dance in love, forevermore.
With every breath, we hear the sound,
Of life divine on holy ground.

The Altar of New Beginnings

Each dawn unfolds a brand new page,
A canvas bright, a chance to stage.
With hearts prepared for what may be,
We stand in faith, we seek to see.

The altar set with dreams and hopes,
In prayerful silence, our spirit copes.
With every tear, we shed the past,
For new beginnings, love will last.

In humble offerings, we lay it down,
The burdens heavy, the worn-out crown.
With open hands, we choose to grow,
Embracing change, as rivers flow.

The sacred cycles teach us well,
In letting go, we break the shell.
A journey forward, bright and bold,
With stories whispered, new and old.

Together we stand, unbroken, free,
In the altar of new beginnings, we see.
Embracing the dawn, we rise and shine,
In love's embrace, forever divine.

Echoes of the Eternal Promise

In echoes soft, the promise calls,
Resounding still, through ancient walls.
The whispers borne on winds of time,
In every heart, a sacred rhyme.

A bond unbroken, strong and true,
In moments shared, me and you.
With every prayer, the spirits weave,
A tapestry of hope, believe.

In silent dawns and dusks of gold,
The stories of the faithful told.
Through trials fierce and joys profound,
The echoes dance, they know no bound.

With every heartbeat, the promise stays,
In love's embrace, we find our ways.
Together bound, we journey on,
Through shadows deep, towards the dawn.

In every whisper, every tear,
We grasp the truth, we hold it near.
In echoes of the eternal grace,
We find our home, our sacred place.

Surrendering to Divine Flow

In whispers of the evening light,
We find a path, serene and bright.
Our burdens cast upon the sea,
In faith, we rest, eternally free.

With open hearts, we yield our will,
The gentle breeze, a sacred thrill.
As rivers merge with ocean vast,
We trust in love that holds us fast.

From troubled shores to tranquil dreams,
We flow with grace in Heaven's beams.
Embracing all, our spirits soar,
In unity, we seek the core.

Each tear a prayer, each smile a vow,
We lift our gaze, surrender now.
Beneath the stars, our souls align,
In harmony, we taste the divine.

The Awakening of the Heart's Voyage

Through silent nights, the heart does stir,
Awakening whispers in the blur.
A journey starts within the chest,
On waves of hope, we sail for rest.

With every breath, the flame ignites,
Illuminating darkest nights.
A tapestry of love we weave,
In trust, we dare to truly believe.

The compass guides with gentle hand,
To shores of grace, we understand.
Each step a lesson, each turn a gift,
In faith, our troubled hearts uplift.

Through storms of doubt, our spirits rise,
We seek the truth that never lies.
With open arms, we greet the dawn,
In unity, forever drawn.

The Light that Guides Our Way

A morning sun breaks through the gray,
Sowing hope along the way.
With each new ray, a promise made,
We follow where the heart has laid.

In shadows deep, we find our spark,
A guiding flame amidst the dark.
With every challenge, courage grows,
In the light, our spirit glows.

Together traversing paths unknown,
We cherish seeds of love that's sown.
In harmony, our voices rise,
A symphony that never dies.

Through valleys low and mountains high,
We journey forth, our spirits fly.
With trust in heart, we make our way,
For light will guide, come what may.

Echoes of Faith in Movement

In silent prayers, our souls engage,
Each heartbeat writes a sacred page.
In rhythms deep, the spirit sways,
Echoes of faith in endless ways.

We dance in circles, hand in hand,
With every step, together stand.
Embraced by love, we feel the call,
In every rise, we will not fall.

Through trials faced, we find our voice,
In unity, we make the choice.
With open hearts, we greet the dawn,
In every moment, we are drawn.

As seasons change, our spirits weave,
In faith's embrace, we dare believe.
With every echo, life shall flow,
In sacred dance, we find our glow.

In the Garden of New Beginnings

In the dawn's soft light we stand,
Whispers of hope fill the air,
Each petal blooms by God's own hand,
Embraced by grace, we share.

The soil rich with dreams to sow,
With every tear, the seeds of love,
In faith, we trust the growth will show,
Guided by stars above.

Together, we shall walk this path,
With hearts ignited by His flame,
In every joy, through every wrath,
We'll honor His holy name.

The waters cleanse our weary souls,
As we journey hand in hand,
In harmony, the spirit rolls,
A chorus across the land.

In this garden, we are reborn,
Each moment ripe with endless grace,
From brokenness, our hearts are worn,
Yet, we find our rightful place.

The Promise of Unfolding

In twilight's glow, a promise grows,
Whispers of truth in the breeze,
Beneath the stars, where love bestows,
A light that bends on knees.

The petals curl to catch the sun,
Reaching out to the sky so wide,
With every dawn, new battles won,
In Him, we shall abide.

In silence deep, His voice we hear,
A melody of peace and trust,
Each moment filled with love, sincere,
In God’s hands, we shall adjust.

Through storms that test our weary hearts,
We cling to faith, a guiding spark,
With every trial, new strength imparts,
Illuminating the dark.

With open arms, we shall embrace,
The promises of days to come,
In kindness found, in His sweet grace,
The world shall know His kingdom's hum.

Grace Invites Us Forward

With every step, His grace we find,
Echoing softly, love calls near,
Through valleys low, with hearts aligned,
In faith, we cast aside our fear.

The road may twist, the path unsure,
Yet hope is woven in our thread,
In trials faced, our souls grow pure,
For in His love, by mercy led.

Each breath we take, a chance to share,
The stories crafted by His hand,
In every moment, found in prayer,
Together, we shall boldly stand.

Through shadows cast, our spirits soar,
As light invites us to explore,
With hearts aflame, we. shall implore,
To reach the heights, forevermore.

Grace, our compass, leads us home,
With every heartbeat, we shall trust,
In unity, we’re never alone,
Together, bound by love's sweet gust.

The Altar of Tomorrow

At the dawn of hope, we gather here,
In humble awe, our prayers arise,
With every whisper, we draw near,
To seek His will beyond the skies.

The altar stands, a sacred space,
For dreams unspoken, yet believed,
We lay our burdens, seek His grace,
In every heart, a love conceived.

Through trials faced, we learn to grow,
With hands outstretched, we find our way,
In fellowship, together we sow,
The seeds of love in warm sunlight's play.

Tomorrow waits with open arms,
A canvas fresh, for us to paint,
With every brush, new earth charms,
In love, we shun the world's complaint.

With faith ablaze, we write our song,
A hymn of hope, forever strong,
In unity, we will belong,
At the altar where we grow along.

Morning Prayers on Fresh Soil

O Lord, the dawn breaks anew,
With whispers of grace in the air.
We gather in the soft dew,
The earth welcomes our fervent prayer.

In silence, we seek Your light,
Where shadows once lingered in gloom.
Blessed are we, in heart and sight,
As hope fills every room.

Each seed of faith we sow today,
Rests gently in the embrace of soil.
As rays warm our humble way,
We trust in Your holy toil.

With hands outstretched, we shall grow,
In unity, we find our call.
Your love, a constant flow,
Through trials that make us whole.

Let us rise, our spirits soar,
In harmony, we lift our song.
With each step, we find the door,
To Your grace, where we belong.

The Pilgrim's Embrace

With every step upon this path,
A journey shared, both far and near.
We walk with faith, escaping wrath,
Embraced by love, we have no fear.

The stars above a guiding light,
Reminding us of grace divine.
Through valleys dark and peaks so bright,
Our hearts entwined, a sacred sign.

In moments fraught with doubt and strife,
We find the strength to carry on.
Your presence, Lord, sustains our life,
In bonds of faith, we are reborn.

The road unfolds, a tapestry,
Woven with threads of every prayer.
In every soul, a destiny,
Together we rise, brighter air.

So let us walk, our spirits free,
In every heart, Your love we trace.
An endless quest, as it should be,
In each embrace, a holy grace.

Light’s New Revelation

Awake, O heart, to dawning light,
A vision rare, pure and profound.
Divine whispers dispel the night,
In grace and truth, our souls are found.

The heavens sing in harmony,
As shadows flee from sacred ground.
In every breath, a symphony,
The promise of a love unbound.

In stillness, we behold the truth,
Unveiling mysteries of the divine.
Each moment sparkles with our youth,
In faith’s embrace, our hearts align.

With every dawn, a chance is born,
To carry forth a light so bright.
In gratitude, we face the morn,
Transformed anew by holy sight.

As rays of hope pour from above,
We walk as vessels of Your grace.
In every soul, a glimpse of love,
In unity, we find our place.

Boundless Horizons of Faith

On wings of prayer, we take to flight,
Beyond the bounds of earthly care.
In endless skies, we find the light,
As faith ignites the heart laid bare.

Through storms and trials, we stand tall,
Our spirits strong, unwavering.
In every challenge, hear the call,
To trust in love, our souls are clinging.

Each horizon holds a promise true,
In courage born of trials faced.
With hearts aflame, we journey through,
In sacred dreams, we find our grace.

Together, we cross every line,
Embracing what the future brings.
With every step, our hearts entwine,
In joyous hope, the spirit sings.

So let us soar to heavens fair,
In unity, our paths entwined.
In every breath, a sacred prayer,
Boundless horizons, faith defined.

When Faith Beckons Forward

In moments dark, when doubts arise,
The light within begins to rise.
With whispered prayer and hopeful heart,
We gather strength, we shall not part.

Each step we take, a path we find,
Guided by grace, our souls aligned.
With open hands and faith anew,
The dawn breaks forth, our spirits true.

Through trials faced, we learn to see,
The deeper truth that sets us free.
In every tear and every smile,
Faith beckons forward all the while.

Together bound, we journey on,
Embracing light, embracing dawn.
No fear can break the holy tie,
With faith as wings, we learn to fly.

So heed the call, let spirits soar,
For in the heart, we find the score.
When faith beckons, we will rise,
Eternal grace beneath the skies.

From Ashes to Ascension

From ashes cold, a flame ignites,
A spirit born, on wings of nights.
In darkened depths, new life will bloom,
Transforming grief into sweet perfume.

With every trial, a chance to rise,
The sacred truth, our hearts surmise.
From shattered dreams, we craft anew,
The path of love will see us through.

In silence deep, the soul will find,
The gentle whispers of the divine.
With every breath, a sacred vow,
From ashes to ascension, take a bow.

As stars align, we feel the call,
Together strong, we will not fall.
In unity, our spirits bend,
To rise with grace, our journey penned.

So let us soar, let hearts be free,
From ashes to the endless sea.
For in the light, we find our song,
In love eternal, we belong.

Rebirth in Sacred Silence

In sacred silence, life begins,
A dance of shadows, light that spins.
Hearts entwined in whispered prayer,
We find rebirth in love's sweet care.

Through quietude, the soul takes flight,
In stillness dwells the purest light.
Each moment filled with grace divine,
Awakening the heart's design.

With every breath, a promise made,
In sacred space, our fears allayed.
From silence blooms, a vibrant song,
In unity, we all belong.

So let us seek the calm within,
Where love abounds, and hope begins.
With open hearts, we journey far,
In sacred silence, be our star.

In the stillness, wisdom reigns,
Rebirth in love, our soul’s sustains.
With every heartbeat, life anew,
In sacred silence, we break through.

Steps into the Unseen

With faith as light, we tread the path,
Through valleys deep, beyond the wrath.
Each step we take, a choice to trust,
In unseen hands, we find our just.

The journey calls, though eyes are blind,
In every heart, the truth we find.
Beyond the veil, a world unfolds,
With whispered dreams, our fate beholds.

Through shadows cast, a vision bright,
In sacred stillness, we gain sight.
With courage fierce, we boldly go,
To dance with faith in faith's flow.

Embrace the light, though veiled it seems,
For in the dark, reside our dreams.
With gentle hands, we shape the way,
Steps into the unseen, we'll stay.

So let us walk, with hearts aglow,
In every step, our spirits grow.
For on this path, divinity,
Steps into the unseen, we see.

Reverent Whispers of Tomorrow

In silence deep, where shadows play,
Hope's gentle breath guides the way.
With hands uplifted, hearts align,
We seek the light, the pure divine.

Each prayer a seed in fertile ground,
In faith's embrace, our souls are found.
The dawn shall break, the night shall flee,
A chorus sings of destiny.

In reverence, we bow our heads,
With open hearts, our spirit spreads.
The whispers of tomorrow call,
In unity, we rise, we fall.

Through trials faced, in love we soar,
The mystic path forevermore.
In every tear, a lesson learned,
With every flame, our passion burned.

Together, hand in hand, we strive,
In sacred bonds, our spirits thrive.
For in this journey, true and pure,
The whispers guide, the heart is sure.

Beneath the Skies of Promise

Beneath the skies where dreams are spun,
The sun shall rise, the dark be done.
In faith, we find our guiding star,
Together, near, though far apart.

The clouds may gather, storms may roar,
Yet love remains an open door.
With every sigh, a prayer is sent,
In sacred moments, hearts are meant.

Through trials faced, our spirits sing,
In hope's embrace, we take to wing.
With eyes uplifted to the skies,
We see the light, the love that lies.

For every shadow cast at dawn,
A promise blooms, a love reborn.
In whispers soft, our souls unite,
Beneath the vast, eternal light.

In circles drawn, our hearts align,
Together we walk, our paths entwined.
In every breath, the sacred flows,
Beneath the skies, our promise grows.

The Mystic’s Journey Beyond

In twilight's glow, the mystic roams,
Through shifting sands, he calls us home.
With every step, a vision clear,
In solitude, we draw so near.

Across the valleys, high and low,
The light of faith begins to glow.
Each mountain climbed, each river crossed,
In seeking truth, we find what’s lost.

The stars above, a guiding hand,
In every heartbeat, we understand.
The journey leads to realms of grace,
In love’s embrace, we find our place.

With open hearts, the mystic sings,
Of all the joy true love can bring.
In sacred whispers, wisdom flows,
Through every trial, the spirit grows.

Awake, arise, the call is near,
In every breath, dissolve the fear.
For in the journey, there’s a home,
A timeless truth, we’re never alone.

Embracing the Divine Narrative

In stories told, the divine unfolds,
In every heart, a truth that holds.
With open arms, we clasp the light,
In sacred bonds, we find our sight.

Each chapter writes a tale of grace,
In trials faced, we find our place.
With words of love, the path is clear,
Embracing all, we hold so dear.

Through every sorrow, joy will rise,
In every tear, a bright disguise.
The narrative we share is vast,
In unity, we bridge the past.

A tapestry of souls entwined,
With every thread, the love we find.
Together woven, stories sing,
In every heart, the joy they bring.

So let us dance where hope ignites,
In rhythms soft, as day turns night.
For in this journey, love will guide,
Embracing all, with arms spread wide.

A Journey Beyond the Veil

In shadows deep, the spirits dwell,
Seeking truths, they weave their spell.
With whispered prayers that rise like smoke,
We tread the path, where silence spoke.

Beyond the veil, the light does shine,
In realms where love and grace entwine.
Each heart a lantern, guiding home,
Through sacred whispers, we shall roam.

The stars above, a sacred map,
In faith we trust, no worldly trap.
With every step, the echoes call,
In unity we rise or fall.

Time stands still, as shadows fade,
In God's embrace, our fears are laid.
With open hearts, we find our way,
In peace and light, we choose to stay.

A journey vast, a quest divine,
Through trials fierce, our spirits shine.
In love's embrace, we finally see,
The journey ends, we're truly free.

Emissaries of the Divine

We walk the earth, with hearts aflame,
Emissaries, in His name.
Each step we take, a sacred vow,
To share His love, to teach us how.

In moments still, the Spirit speaks,
Through gentle smiles and humble deeds.
We lift the weary, we heal the pain,
As vessels of grace, in joy we reign.

The world may be dark, but we bring light,
With faith as our armor, we embrace the fight.
In every soul, His image shines,
With open hands, His love entwines.

Together we rise, united strong,
In harmony, we sing our song.
Through trials faced and prayers poured forth,
We honor the light, our holy worth.

In fields of plenty, our labor blooms,
In hearts that gather, His sweet perfumes.
Emissaries sent, to spread His peace,
With every whisper, let worries cease.

Wings of the Redeemed

Awake, O soul, to truth divine,
With wings of grace, together we climb.
Through trials faced and shadows cast,
We soar above the storms that last.

In every heart, a sacred spark,
Illuminates the path through dark.
With every breath, redemption sings,
A symphony of grace that brings.

The burden light, the spirit free,
In faith we find our clarity.
As whispers guide, we dance in light,
The wings of hope take wondrous flight.

Together we rise, the redeemed stand tall,
In unity we answer the call.
For every wound that love has healed,
The promise of joy is then revealed.

With open eyes and hearts aflame,
We journey forth, proclaim His name.
With every step, the heavens cheer,
As angels gather, drawing near.

The Embrace of the Eternal

In quiet moments, souls entwine,
The sacred bond, both yours and mine.
In serene stillness, we find our place,
Within the arms of His embrace.

Through seasons change, the love remains,
In joy and sorrow, in laughter, pains.
With faces turned to heaven high,
We find our truth, we learn to fly.

Each prayer a thread, a tapestry spun,
Connecting hearts, our battles won.
In unity, we breathe as one,
In His embrace, the race is run.

Time may falter, but love remains,
In every life, His spirit reigns.
Through every trial, we seek the light,
In His embrace, we find our flight.

The eternal bond, a sacred flow,
In peace we gather, in love we grow.
Beyond the veil, we'll meet once more,
In His embrace, forever soar.

Threads of Faith Woven Anew

In the tapestry of life we stand,
Each thread a whisper of His hand.
With colors bright and stories told,
Our hearts entwined, in faith we hold.

Through trials faced, we seek the light,
In shadows deep, He guides our sight.
With every stitch, hope's fabric grows,
In unity, His love bestows.

From doubt to trust, we journey on,
By grace embraced, till fear is gone.
Each prayer a knot, in peace we bind,
In sacred space, His truth we find.

The loom of life, where souls embrace,
In woven strength, we find our place.
With every heartbeat, spirits soar,
Threads of faith, forevermore.

Let us rejoice in this design,
For love unites, and hearts align.
As paths entwine, we walk as one,
In faith's embrace, our journey's begun.

Rising with the Morning Star

A new day breaks, the light appears,
With gentle grace, He calms our fears.
The dawn's embrace, so warm and bright,
In silence speaks His love and might.

With every breath, our spirits rise,
We find our strength in endless skies.
The morning star, a guiding flame,
Reminding us we are all the same.

In prayerful whispers, hearts take flight,
Embracing hope that banishes night.
With gratitude, we greet the morn,
In every beat, His love reborn.

The world awakens, sings His praise,
Each moment shines in sacred ways.
Together we stand, hand in hand,
Unified in faith's strong band.

Let our hearts be filled with light,
As we journey through day and night.
With every sunrise, blessings flow,
In Him we trust, and love we sow.

The Transformation of the Heart

In quiet moments, change begins,
As light invades, the darkness thins.
A heart once lost, now finds its song,
In love's embrace, we all belong.

With every tear, a seed we sow,
In trials faced, His grace will grow.
Transforming pain to purest gold,
In depths of sorrow, love unfolds.

From ashes rise, the spirits lift,
Renewed in faith, a sacred gift.
In unity, our hearts will share,
The beauty found in answered prayer.

With open hands, we offer trust,
In every heart, His love is just.
As chains are broken, freedom's near,
In transformation, we persevere.

So let the heart, once hard as stone,
Be softened now, and thus made known.
In love's embrace, we find our part,
A journey true, the transformed heart.

Blessings Unfolding Like Petals

In gardens rich, we see His grace,
Each blessing blooms, a sacred space.
Like petals soft, they come alive,
With every dawn, our spirits strive.

As nature's hand, in tender care,
Helps us to bloom, to love, to share.
With colors bright, our souls ignite,
In faith's embrace, we find our light.

With gentle whispers, breezes flow,
In each unfolding, blessings grow.
The fragrance sweet, of love bestowed,
In every heart, His truth is sowed.

So let us walk through fields of grace,
Where every step, our dreams embrace.
In unity, we share the load,
With open hearts, love's path is showed.

In sacred gardens, let us dwell,
For blessings come, and all is well.
As petals fall, new blooms arise,
In life's great dance, our spirits rise.

Songs of Renewal and Grace

Whispers of light in the dawn,
Hearts uplifted, burdens gone.
In His embrace, we find our way,
Guided by love, come what may.

Beauty in the simplest things,
Hope anew, as nature sings.
Grace descends like morning dew,
Restoration, pure and true.

Faith, a river flowing free,
Cleansed and washed, eternally.
Every tear a seed of change,
In the heart, we rearrange.

Let the shadows fade away,
Breath divine at close of day.
In surrender, we are whole,
Awakening the gentle soul.

Celebrate the gift of fire,
Yearning souls that never tire.
Renewal in the trials faced,
Life's journey, woven, graced.

The Shifting Tides of the Soul

Waves of doubt crash on the shore,
Yet faith anchors, evermore.
Tides that rise and tides that fall,
In His love, we find our call.

Whispers drift upon the breeze,
Carrying dreams, hearts at ease.
Change is constant, yet so dear,
Guiding us through every fear.

In the depths, seek and you'll find,
Truth in whispers, pure, unblind.
Gentle strength in every shift,
Spirit's grace, our sacred gift.

As the moon guides ocean's dance,
So are we, in love's expanse.
Trust the journey of the heart,
In the ebb and flow, we start.

Let the currents wash away,
Sins of yesterday, dismay.
Embrace the waves of compassion,
In His arms, find our passion.

Harvesting Blessings Yet-to-Come

Fields of plenty stretch afar,
Beneath the sun, a shining star.
With faithful hands, we toil and sow,
Trusting in grace, our blessings grow.

Seeds of hope, in soil they rest,
To yield the fruits, they are blessed.
Patience we learn, in silence deep,
Through darkest nights, our faith we keep.

Rays of dawn bring light anew,
Promises kept, in skies so blue.
Harvest fields, a bountiful grace,
In every heart, His warm embrace.

Gathering joy, soul's deep delight,
In community, we share the light.
Work as one, our hands unite,
Fostering love, in faith, ignite.

Each blessing feels, yet to unfold,
Stories of love, eternally told.
In the garden of our holy ground,
Together, hope and peace are found.

Sowing Seeds of Spiritual Growth

In the stillness, seeds are sown,
Faith takes root in hearts unknown.
Nurtured by prayer, hope, and grace,
Sprouting forth, a holy space.

Tend the garden, let time unfold,
Miracles bloom, stories told.
From little things, great wonders rise,
In every soul, love never dies.

Patience, a virtue we must learn,
Through trials faced, we start to yearn.
For deeper truths, our spirits seek,
In silence, wisdom's voice will speak.

With every burden, lightened load,
We gather strength upon this road.
Walk in faith, the journey long,
In unity, we find the song.

Harvest seasons, ripe and blessed,
In every heart, His love invests.
Sow with joy, our glorious chance,
Trust in Him, and join the dance.

Dawn of the Believer

In the hush of morn, we rise anew,
Faith like the sun, breaking through.
Promises whispered in the early light,
Hearts awakened to a holy sight.

With every step, the Spirit leads,
Guiding us gently, planting seeds.
Trust in His path, our doubts must cease,
Find in His arms a perfect peace.

Mountains bow low, and valleys sing,
Joy in the journey, hope’s gentle spring.
Hands lifted high, voices in praise,
For we are His love; our lives He'll raise.

The morning star shines bright above,
A reminder of His endless love.
In the dawn, our hearts ignite,
Forever bound in pure delight.

Let faith be the anchor, strong and true,
For every storm, He’ll guide us through.
With eyes fixed high, we will not stray,
In the dawn of grace, we find our way.

The Covenant Renewed

Upon the altar, promises made,
In the stillness, His grace displayed.
With hands outstretched, we bow in awe,
A testament of faith in every law.

The heavens whisper, a sacred pact,
In every heartbeat, a holy act.
Through trials faced and joy bestowed,
Together we walk on this winding road.

From ashes rising, hopes emerge,
In the light of love, we find our urge.
Hearts entwined in a divine embrace,
With every moment, we seek His face.

Mighty are His ways, steadfast and true,
Each promise kept, a covenant renewed.
In unity we stand, hand in hand,
A family bound by His command.

The journey unfolds with every breath,
In joy and sorrow, life and death.
For He is our guide, our Savior and King,
In the covenant of love, we forever cling.

Pages of Grace Unfolding

In the book of life, the pages turn,
Stories told of love we yearn.
Each chapter inked with trials faced,
In His embrace, we find our place.

With wisdom's ink, our paths are drawn,
In every dusk, behold the dawn.
The lessons learned in tearful eyes,
Reveal the blessings in disguise.

He writes our tales with gentle hands,
In every sorrow, a promise stands.
Turning struggle into grace,
In the landscape of His embrace.

Voices lifted, hymns arise,
In grateful hearts, our spirits fly.
Pages of grace, forever penned,
A story of hope that will never end.

In every heartbeat, divine design,
Each moment sacred, love divine.
As we walk this path of light,
The pages unfold towards His height.

Light Through the Shadows

In shadows deep, His light breaks through,
A beacon bright, forever true.
With every step, we feel His hand,
Guiding our hearts through a barren land.

Fear not the night, for dawn will come,
His mercy flows like a gentle hum.
In darkest valleys, we find our song,
Together in faith, we all belong.

The light descends, illuminating grace,
Each tear we shed, a holy trace.
Transformed by love, we rise anew,
In the glow of His light, we are made true.

Hope like a phoenix will take its flight,
Through every conflict, our spirits ignite.
In unity we shine, a radiant spark,
Guided by faith, we conquer the dark.

Hold fast to love, let it be your guide,
In every shadow, let faith abide.
For even in trials, His light we'll see,
Through shadows we walk, forever free.

Embrace of the Unseen Path

In shadows deep, the spirit roams,
Guided by light, yet unseen domes.
Footsteps follow ancient ways,
In silence, find the heart's true gaze.

The road winds on, a sacred thread,
With faith as compass, we are led.
Each twist reveals the hidden grace,
In every heart, His love we trace.

Winds of change whisper soft and low,
Beneath the surface, rivers flow.
Trust the journey, hand in hand,
In unity, together we stand.

The unseen path, a blessing pure,
Through trials steep, our souls endure.
With every step, the spirit glows,
In darkness bright, our faith bestows.

Embrace the grace of every hour,
In moments small, we find His power.
For in the unseen lies the key,
To live in love, eternally free.

Revelation in the Quiet

In the stillness, truth unfolds,
A gentle whisper, love retold.
In solitude, we find our peace,
The heart's soft song will never cease.

Beneath the stars, we seek the light,
Illuminating the darkest night.
Silent prayers ascend like smoke,
In every breath, His love awoke.

When worldly noise begins to fade,
The soul finds joy in silence made.
In moments quiet, we can see,
The vastness of divinity.

Soft hues of dawn, a sacred call,
In every shadow, His grace falls.
From quiet hearts, pure revelations,
We rise to meet our true foundations.

In gentle waves, the spirit sways,
In hushed reflections, truth conveys.
Revelation waits in every sigh,
In quietude, we learn to fly.

The Faithful Journey Ahead

The road before us stretches wide,
With every heartbeat, faith our guide.
Through valleys low and mountains steep,
In every challenge, promises keep.

With open hearts, we take the leap,
In trust we stand, in hope we weep.
For every step holds sacred grace,
In trials met, His love we face.

The faithful journey knows no end,
In every stranger, a hidden friend.
Compassion blooms along the way,
In every dawn, anew we pray.

Though storms may rage, our spirits soar,
In unity, we find the door.
To paths unknown, we must abide,
With faith as anchor, love our guide.

With courage bright, we journey on,
In every dusk, a promise drawn.
The faithful heart will never tire,
In love's embrace, we lift our choir.

The journey calls, take heed and tread,
With every whisper, He has led.
Together strong, we rise above,
In faith we walk, in grace we love.

Whispers of Transformation

In every moment, change will breathe,
With gentle whispers, hearts believe.
A seed of hope begins to swell,
In silence, hear the truth we tell.

The shifting sands beneath our feet,
Remind us that we can repeat.
From ash to flame, the spirit wakes,
Transformation comes, the heart remakes.

In letting go, we find our wings,
In faith renewed, the spirit sings.
Through trials faced, the soul will shine,
In every tear, His love entwined.

Embrace the change, the sacred flow,
In every loss, new seeds will grow.
Whispers of grace in shadows twine,
In every ending, love aligns.

With open arms, we greet the dawn,
In every heartbeat, transformation.
A path of light laid out ahead,
In whispers soft, our spirits wed.

Through every storm, we learn to rise,
In sacred trust, we touch the skies.
Whispers of transformation call,
In unity, we stand, not fall.

Embracing the Call of the Spirit

In quiet whispers, the Spirit calls,
Open hearts where love enthralls.
With gentle hands, it guides our way,
Illuminating night to day.

Through trials faced and burdens borne,
We rise anew, in faith reborn.
Each tear, a drop of sacred grace,
In every struggle, we find our place.

The rhythm of the soul's sweet song,
A melody where we belong.
In stillness, we can hear it near,
The sacred truth that conquers fear.

Embrace the call, let spirits soar,
In unity, we seek for more.
With every breath, His love we claim,
A radiant light that knows our name.

In silent prayer, our spirits rise,
Connected through the endless skies.
A tapestry of hope we weave,
In faith, we stand, in grace, believe.

Illuminating the Path Ahead

Upon the trail, where shadows lay,
The light of truth will guide our way.
Each step we take, a promise shine,
As love unfolds, our hearts align.

In every doubt, the flame ignites,
A beacon bright in darkest nights.
With open eyes, we seek the dawn,
Awakened souls, forever drawn.

The Spirit's voice sings soft and clear,
Leading us through pain and fear.
Illuminating fears inside,
Revelations where hope abides.

With every breath, we journey bold,
In faith, our stories shall unfold.
Together bound, we walk as one,
Towards a light that can't be shun.

Each moment dwells in holy grace,
A journey shared, a warm embrace.
Together we rise, forever free,
In the light of love, in unity.

The Promise of Dawn’s Embrace

When morning breaks, with colors bright,
It whispers hope to greet the light.
The promise of a brand new day,
In dawn’s embrace, we find our way.

With gentle rays, the sun does rise,
Dispelling doubts, dispelling lies.
A canvas pure, our spirits glow,
Awakening the love we know.

In every heart, a yearning grows,
To kneel in faith, and let love flow.
As dawn arrives, we stand renewed,
In gratitude, our souls imbued.

Each heartbeat echoes heaven's song,
In harmony, where we belong.
With every step, the path unfolds,
A tale of grace that love upholds.

As shadows flee and dreams arise,
In unity, we reach the skies.
The promise made, we sing in praise,
For every dawn, our hearts ablaze.

Beyond the Veil of Yesterday

Beyond the veil, where shadows creep,
In sacred stillness, secrets sleep.
The echoes of our past remain,
Yet in the light, we break the chain.

With every scar, a story told,
A testament of love unfolds.
Through trials passed, we seek anew,
A brighter path, a clearer view.

In faith we shed what once was real,
Embracing lessons that we feel.
The Spirit whispers, “Rise and see,
The beauty of your destiny.”

No longer bound by yesterday's chains,
We find our strength where love remains.
With open hearts, we walk this way,
In unity, we greet the day.

For every tear that fell in pain,
A seed of hope begins to gain.
With every dawn, new life we bring,
Beyond the veil, our spirits sing.

Dances with Destiny

In silence waits the heart of man,
To heed the call of destiny's plan.
With open arms and fervent grace,
We twirl beneath the stars we chase.

In shadows cast, our doubts align,
Yet faith ignites, our spirits shine.
The path unfolds, it's ours to take,
In every step, a bond we make.

With whispers soft, the angels sing,
Guiding us through everything.
Embrace the chance, let courage rise,
For in our dance, the truth lies.

We twine with fate, a sacred trust,
In every moment, in God we must.
Together we weave a tapestry,
Of light and love, eternally.

So let us dance, our souls entwined,
Forever seeking, forever blind.
In unity, we find our way,
Dances with destiny, come what may.

Ascending the Ladder of Faith

With every rung, the spirit soars,
Each step, a prayer that ever roars.
Upward we climb, toward the divine,
In the light of hope, our hearts align.

The struggles faced, the burdens shared,
In moments of doubt, we are prepared.
Each faith-filled step, a sacred trust,
We rise together, it's God we must.

Hand in hand, we seek the flame,
The ladder beckons, calling our name.
With every reach, our purpose clear,
Destined to rise, we conquer fear.

The heights we gain, through grace bestowed,
In love and mercy, our spirits flowed.
Each view embraced, a vision bright,
Ascending faith, our guiding light.

So challenge despair, let courage lead,
For in our climb, we plant the seed.
In unity forged, our future awaits,
Ascending the ladder, where destiny gates.

Uncharted Waters of the Soul

In the depths of silence, we embark,
To navigate the waters, deep and stark.
With faith as our compass, we'll never stray,
In uncharted realms, we find our way.

The waves may clash, the storms may roar,
Yet in our hearts, we seek for more.
Through shadows thick, and whispers thin,
The voyage calls our souls within.

Each drop of grace like morning dew,
Refreshes us, makes us anew.
In every tide, a lesson waits,
In uncharted waters, God creates.

We sail along, through trials vast,
Gathering strength from lessons past.
In unity, we'll chart the course,
Our spirits freed by love's true force.

So let us dive into the deep,
And trust the journey, ours to keep.
In uncharted waters, we rise and flow,
For the soul's true depth is what we sow.

The Blessed Threshold

Before the door of grace we stand,
A sacred space, a guiding hand.
With faith in heart, and hope in sight,
We ready ourselves for sacred light.

In the silence, the whispers call,
A gentle nudge, a loving thrall.
With open hearts, we step inside,
Into the warmth where love abides.

Each threshold crossed, a promise made,
In every moment, fear will fade.
The blessings flow, a river vast,
In unity born from shadows cast.

So linger not in doubts of old,
For in this space, our hearts unfold.
With trust unwavering, the journey starts,
The blessed threshold, a home for hearts.

Together we rise, in purpose clear,
Embracing love, conquering fear.
In gratitude, we find our place,
The blessed threshold, our sacred space.

Beneath the Canopy of Divine Will

In shadows deep, the heavens greet,
A guiding hand in life's heartbeat.
We walk beneath a sacred glow,
In every moment, love will flow.

Wisdom whispers through the trees,
In silent prayer, our souls find ease.
Each leaf a prayer, each breeze a song,
In unity, we all belong.

The stars above, a map so bright,
They lead us through the darkest night.
With every step, our spirits rise,
Beneath this canopy, we prize.

Together in this sacred space,
We seek the truth, we find His grace.
With open hearts, we humbly stand,
Connected by His loving hand.

Our voices lift, in harmony,
In gratitude, we bow the knee.
For life's a gift, a sacred trust,
In Divine will, we place our must.

Anointed by the Light of Tomorrow

In dawn's embrace, the spirit wakes,
A promise shines, a hope that stakes.
With each new ray, our hearts ignite,
Anointed by the purest light.

Through trials faced and mountains climbed,
Our souls are forged, our lives aligned.
With faith the flame, we bravely tread,
Where'er we wander, He has led.

The path is clear, though shadows fall,
In every struggle, He hears our call.
With resilience born from love divine,
We walk in grace, our lives entwined.

As seasons turn and moments flow,
Our spirits grow, and love will show.
With hands uplifted, hearts aglow,
We are the seeds of tomorrow's show.

In prayerful breath, we find our way,
Through every night and brightening day.
Anointed souls, forever free,
In His embrace, our destiny.

Dance of the Soul's Renewal

In sacred rhythm, hearts align,
A dance of grace, a love divine.
With every step, we shed the past,
In joy we find the breath of vast.

The whispers of the ancient song,
Unite our spirits, make us strong.
In circles spun of hope and light,
We twirl together, pure delight.

The journey deep, the path unclear,
But faith ignites what we hold dear.
With open arms, we embrace change,
In this dance, we find what's strange.

Each leap of faith, each gentle sway,
Renews the spirit, guides our way.
Through trials faced, through love we find,
A dance of souls, forever kind.

In twilight's glow, we spin and sing,
With hearts awakened, hope we bring.
The dance of life, a sacred call,
Together we rise, together we fall.

The Covenant of Growth and Giving

In fields of grace, we plant our seed,
With open hands, we share the need.
For every harvest blossoms here,
In love we grow, in faith we steer.

Bound by the vow of giving light,
We walk together, hearts ignite.
Through trials faced and burdens shared,
In this covenant, we are bared.

Each act of kindness, a thread of gold,
We weave a tapestry, life behold.
With every gesture, every prayer,
The tapestry grows, beyond compare.

In community, our spirits thrive,
Through love and care, we're kept alive.
For what we give, we shall receive,
In unity, we shall believe.

As seasons change and moments flow,
The spirit of giving starts to glow.
In this sacred pact, we all align,
The covenant of growth, divine.

The Eternal Dance of Becoming

In the dawn of creation, we rise,
Whispers of angels, under vast skies.
Each heartbeat a promise, each step a grace,
In the sacred rhythm, we find our place.

With shadows and light, we intertwine,
Evolving in love, through every design.
The cosmos spins, a tapestry bright,
Unfolding our souls in eternal light.

We dance through the ages, in joy and in pain,
Like waves on the shore, we come back again.
In the embrace of the infinite sea,
We are but reflections of the divine decree.

In unity's circle, we gather and weave,
The stories of many, the dreams we believe.
With each turn of fate, our spirits advance,
In harmony's song, we continue our dance.

As stardust we wander, as brothers, as kin,
In the heart of the world, our journey begins.
The eternal dance beckons, hear its sweet sound,
In the arms of the cosmos, true peace can be found.

Walking Through the Sacred Threshold

At the edge of the world, we pause and reflect,
On the journey behind, with all its effect.
A veil softly lifts, the spirits align,
Inviting the seeker to step out of time.

With hearts full of courage, we breathe in the air,
Embracing the moment, shedding all fear.
The path to the light is both narrow and wide,
Each footfall a promise on this sacred ride.

In the silence, we hear the echoes of truth,
As the whispers of wisdom reveal joys of youth.
A threshold once crossed, a new light appears,
With each step forward, we dance through our tears.

Through valleys of shadows, to mountains of grace,
We find our way home in this holy space.
The road may be winding, but faith is the guide,
As we walk through the threshold, with love by our side.

And when we look back on the steps that we've trod,
We'll see the reflections of the face of God.
In the sacredness found, in the tales we unfold,
We walk through the threshold, our spirits consoled.

Arrivals in Places Unknown

Under the stars, we journey afar,
With dreams as our compass, we follow the spar.
In places unknown, where the heart truly sees,
We find our horizons, in whispers of trees.

The valleys may beckon, the mountains may call,
With each new horizon, we lean into all.
The laughter of children, the songs of the wise,
In each fleeting moment, new visions arise.

With feet on the path and minds open wide,
We gather the wisdom the universe provides.
Through trials and triumphs, we grow and we learn,
In the fire of living, our spirits will burn.

Though faced with the storms, we rise above fear,
The light of the sacred will always be near.
In arrivals we find what was lost in our roam,
In the heart of the journey, we discover our home.

So let us embrace every turn of the key,
In the wonder of life, forever we'll be.
With open hearts traveling, together we're grown,
In the dance of the life, we are never alone.

The Language of Transformation

In the silence of night, a heartbeat speaks,
To the soul's deepest yearnings, the spirit seeks.
With each breath a canvas, colors arise,
In the act of transforming, the soul never lies.

Through shadows of doubt, we learn to ascend,
In the chrysalis' warmth, the heart will amend.
With whispers of love, the old fades away,
As the dawn of the new brings forth bright day.

The petals fall gently, an offering pure,
In vulnerability, our strength will endure.
A symphony plays in the depths of our heart,
In the dance of becoming, we all play a part.

Each lesson a treasure, each loss a gain,
Through the rivers of sorrow, we learn to sustain.
With faith as our anchor, we flow without fear,
In the language of truth, our purpose is clear.

So let us rejoice in this sacred exchange,
As we navigate paths, both strange and deranged.
In the tapestry woven by hands so divine,
We find our true essence, in the grand design.

Deep Calls to Deep

In the stillness of the night,
Hearts whisper praise to the skies.
Depths of soul seek deeper light,
In the silence, the spirit flies.

Waves of mercy wash the shore,
Binding all the lost and found.
In this ocean, we implore,
Peace resounding all around.

From the depths, rich prayers ascend,
Carried forth on holy air.
In our longing, we depend,
On the love that’s always there.

Echoes of a sacred call,
Bringing hope in darkest night.
Let our hearts respond, not fall,
To the depths of pure delight.

In the quiet, we may see,
All the wonders grace reveals.
In this place, we're truly free,
Deep calls to deep, our soul heals.

Rebirth in Sacred Silence

In the hush of morning glow,
Broken spirits find their grace.
From the stillness seeds will grow,
In the heart, we find our place.

Muted cries, a tender prayer,
Whispers dance on softest breeze.
In the silence, we declare,
Faithful trust brings us to peace.

Life emerges from the dark,
In the womb of quiet dawn.
Every heartbeat bears a mark,
Of a love that carries on.

Through the stillness, hear the song,
Echoes of the Divine tune.
In the silence, we belong,
Cradled by the brightening moon.

Rebirth comes in sacred space,
Where the spirit breathes anew.
Every thought a soft embrace,
In the silence, we find true.

The Shepherd's New Song

With a gentle hand, He leads,
Softly calls each wandering heart.
In His care, the soul proceeds,
Finding peace, a brand new start.

Through the valleys, shadows cast,
Fear dissolves in His true light.
All our burdens, left in past,
In His presence, we take flight.

Listen close to every note,
He sings love, bright as the day.
In our hearts, His truth will float,
Guiding us along the way.

Every step, a sacred dance,
In His grace we find our song.
Feel the rhythm, take a chance,
In His shelter, we belong.

The shepherd's voice will never fade,
In our souls, a melody.
By His love, we are remade,
Singing praises, wild and free.

Guideposts of the Faithful

In the trials of this journey,
Hearts unite to seek the way.
With each guidepost, love will burn,
Lighting paths for brighter day.

With every prayer, we find our truth,
In the whispers of despair.
Hope renews the spirit's youth,
Strengthened by the love we share.

Hands that reach will touch the sky,
Faith a compass ever strong.
In our quest, we do not shy,
For together, we belong.

Every stone, a story told,
Marking each step along the way.
With our hearts in faith, we hold,
These guideposts here to light our day.

When the shadows try to creep,
Look for signs of grace and hope.
In our bond, we take a leap,
Guideposts help our spirits cope.

The Sacred Turning

In the stillness of the night,
Whispers echo through the skies.
Hearts unfold, a gentle light,
Leading souls to rise and rise.

With every breath, we seek His grace,
In every challenge, see His face.
A journey that we all must take,
In the sacred turning, we awake.

Harmony flows like a river wide,
Uniting all on this divine ride.
With open arms, we share the way,
Guided by love, come what may.

In the circle, we find the truth,
Bond of spirit, ageless youth.
Together we strive, hand in hand,
To honor the sacred, forever stand.

Let the echoes of faith resound,
In every heart, a sacred ground.
With trust, we turn, we seek the One,
In the sacred turning, we have just begun.

Seeds of Renewal

In the soil where hope is sown,
Miracles bloom, in silence grown.
With every tear, a seed is cast,
A promise that the storm won't last.

Gentle rains wash over dreams,
Sunlight glimmers in golden beams.
From ashes new life shall arise,
Seeds of renewal, reaching the skies.

In the garden of forgotten souls,
Faith takes root, and love consoles.
Together we rise from dust to grace,
In every heart, His warm embrace.

As the seasons dance and turn,
Lessons learned, this hard-earned yearn.
In each moment, His wisdom guides,
With seeds of renewal, hope abides.

So plant the seeds, let them grow,
In every heart, a radiant glow.
In the soil of our being true,
Seeds of renewal, made anew.

The Call to Awakening

Awake, dear soul, to the light,
In shadows deep, there shines a spark.
The universe sings, a sacred rite,
Calling forth the brave from dark.

With every heartbeat, feel the pull,
The whisper of the Divine near.
In the silence, the heart is full,
Awaiting the moment to draw near.

Answer the call that stirs your core,
Embrace the path that lays ahead.
With open eyes, explore and soar,
In love's embrace, your fears are shed.

Light ignites like a candle's flame,
Awakening dreams that long have slept.
In this journey, you are the name,
In unity, the promise kept.

So heed the call, let courage reign,
Every step leads to a new dawn.
In awakening, we break the chain,
Embracing life, reborn, reborn.

Treasures from the Abyss

In depths below, where shadows weave,
Lies the heart of truth concealed.
From the abyss, we learn to grieve,
Yet find treasures, once revealed.

Through trials dark, the soul will grow,
In silence, wisdom finds its way.
Each pain a seed, each tear a flow,
A map of hope in night and day.

From the depths, we rise anew,
Strength forged in challenges faced.
In the abyss, courage grew,
For in darkness, grace is laced.

Seek the gems in every fall,
Lessons gleam in hidden light.
In the journey, hear the call,
From the abyss, we take our flight.

So cherish heartaches, every bruise,
For treasures found, they will not fade.
In the abyss, we choose to choose,
A brighter path, our lives remade.

Milton Keynes UK
Ingram Content Group UK Ltd.
UKHW020041271124
451585UK00012B/977

9 789916 899779